NATIONAL GEOGRAPHIC

PIONEER EDITION

By Michael Ruscoe

CONTENTS

Play B

all!

It has been more than 100 years since the first World Series. So break out the hot dogs, the peanuts—and the stories. Baseball is a great window into America's history.

By Michael Ruscoe

Each summer, 70 million people go to baseball games. What do they see? They see players on the field. But that is not all.

Fans also see American history. Since the 1800s, baseball has grown with the United States. Changes in the sport also show the changes in our country.

3

Civil War Games. *Prisoners of war play baseball in Salisbury, North Carolina.*

War Games

People have played baseball since before the Civil War. This was a war between the states. It began in 1861.

Thirteen states **seceded.** They broke away and formed their own country. The U.S. Army fought to take them back. The war lasted four years.

Soldiers played baseball whenever they could. Prisoners played to keep from getting bored. Sometimes guards played too. The game was a break from the war.

The Civil War ended in 1865. Yet baseball lived on. Soldiers went home. They took baseball with them. The game spread across the country.

Some cities formed two teams. One was for blacks. Another was for whites. Baseball was **segregated,** or divided by people's race. So was the country.

At Bat. *This ball player was on the cover of an 1890 baseball guidebook.*

The National Pastime

Baseball became more and more popular. People began to call it "the national **pastime.**" A pastime is something fun to do.

Many Americans enjoyed the sport. Rich people and poor people watched baseball games. Even U.S. presidents had fun in ballparks. They began many new traditions.

President William H. Taft threw the first pitch of the season in 1910. Woodrow Wilson (right) was the first President to attend a World Series game.

Star-Spangled Sport

In 1917, the United States entered World War I. The war gave many people a sense of **patriotism.** That is a love for one's country.

Americans shared their patriotism at baseball games. They sang "The Star-Spangled Banner" at the start of each game.

A New League

World War II began just 20 years after World War I. The United States entered the war in 1941. Many players left baseball to be soldiers.

While the men were at war, women went to work. They got jobs that had been done only by men. Women also got the chance to play baseball.

The All-American Girls baseball league formed in 1943. The league had many great players. It kept going after the war. But the league closed in 1954. Since then, only men have played professional baseball.

Ending Segregation

Even after World War II, blacks and whites played on different teams. Baseball and America were still segregated. But not for long.

In 1947, Jackie Robinson made history. He became the first black player to join the major leagues. He helped many Americans see that segregation was wrong. A few years later, laws were passed to end segregation in schools.

A World Sport

Today, baseball is still an American pastime. But it is also popular all around the world. People from many countries now play the sport. Some even make it to the major leagues. These players and their fans are part of America's history.

Girl Power. *During the 1940s, ten All-American Girls teams drew about a million fans a year.*

6

Sliding Into Fame. *Jackie Robinson made headlines when he began playing in the majors in 1947. Two years later, he was named Most Valuable Player.*

Wordwise

pastime: fun activity

patriotism: love for one's country

secede: to break away

segregated: divided by race

So Close! *Asia won five straight games in the 2002 Little League World Series. They lost the final game—by one run.*

The Color of Baseball

Making History.
Andrew "Rube" Foster founded the first black baseball league in 1920.

In 1947, Jackie Robinson made history. He joined an all-white baseball team. Yet he was not the first black player to do so.

Bud Fowler joined a white team in 1878. He was the only black player at the time. Soon, there were as many as 50 black players in the league.

Yet by 1900, blacks were banned from white teams. Segregation kept blacks and whites apart. So black players made their own leagues. Andrew "Rube" Foster started the Negro National League in 1920. Soon other black leagues formed.

Playing for Crowds.
Despite segregation, many Negro league games were played in major league stadiums.

Life in the Leagues

The Negro leagues had many fans. Black teams traveled across the United States. They played in small towns and big cities. The players were heroes. Some people dropped everything to see them play.

Black baseball stars did not have it easy. They faced the same problems as blacks around the country. Players could not eat at many restaurants. They could not stay in many hotels. They sometimes slept in their bus. Segregation made their lives hard.

The End of an Era

The major leagues opened to blacks in 1947. Soon all of the black leagues closed. Yet blacks started making history in a new way. They became stars in the major leagues.

On the Road. *Black teams often rode buses on trips across the U.S.*

Superstars of th ★★★★

More than 4,000 people played on Negro league teams. Some of the best have been voted into the National Baseball Hall of Fame.

JAMES "COOL PAPA" BELL

James "Cool Papa" Bell was known as the fastest man in baseball. He could circle the bases in just twelve seconds. His speed let him steal many bases. People say he once stole two bases on a single pitch.

Negro Leagues

SATCHEL PAIGE

atchel Paige played baseball for more than thirty years. He was one of he best pitchers of all time. He was the first Negro league player in the Hall of Fame. He joined the major leagues in 1948. That year, he helped his team win the World Series.

JOSH GIBSON

Josh Gibson was one of the best hitters in black baseball. He could smack the ball more than 500 feet. He hit 962 home runs during his career. Gibson died three months before blacks were allowed to join the major leagues.

Baseball

**Take a crack at these questions
to find out what you learned.**

1 Why did baseball become popular after the Civil War?

2 Why did blacks and whites play on different teams?

3 Why did fans start singing "The Star-Spangled Banner"?

4 Why did the All-American Girls league form?

5 What does baseball show about our country's history?